"An intelligent and gutsy comedy… a subversive detour into the dark side of institutional care… Gee succeeds on every front… a bright, sharp, well-executed, highly thoughtful play that deals with difficult subject matter in a respectful and considerate way, and delivered by a performer who comes off like a stone-cold genius. And with increasing health care spending, shortage of available health care services, and an ever-aging population, the timing couldn't be better… a disturbing masterpiece." Gig City, Alberta

"A remarkable piece of writing… with a few well-chosen phrases, Gee creates fully formed characters that can be a source of pity, exasperation and humor… this murder mystery is also cleverly a comedy, meditation on human dignity and at its heart, a love story… with his shrewd mix of humor and heart, Gee strikes storytelling gold." Orlando Sentinel

"Smart, witty, and razor-sharp… what's most impressive is the way Gee has used the whodunit trope as a way to expose the real-life indignities of living with late stage dementia. Part social commentary, part black comedy, and part Clue… funny and heartbreaking as hell."
Canadian Broadcasting Corporation

"Exceptionally well-constructed comedy/drama with crafty nuances and undertones… the laughs are genuine and well-timed, the drama sneaks up on you and there are wonderful moments of reflection on mortality and morality." UMFM Radio, Manitoba

"A poignant story, cleverly written and performed brilliantly. Gee has taken a very sensitive issue and has created an accessible piece of theatre that is funny, dark and very witty." Purple Revolver, Liverpool

"Very few have the talents of Rob Gee, who manages to pull off a truly wacky show and convey something meaningful at the same time."
Vue Weekly, Alberta

"Humane, informative and entertaining… the characters have remarkable depth." Now Magazine, Toronto

"By turns sad and funny, and just plain fun. This one-man triumph is equal parts mystery, comedy, storytelling, social commentary — and 100 per cent entertaining." Winnipeg Free Press

"A wonderful example of great writing and acting dovetailing to create an all too believable world, where the inherent sadness of lives coming to an end is not without moments of poetry and a vivid reminder that all lives have value and meaning." Theatre in London

"Compelling… unique and fascinating… great writing."
Saskatoon StarPhoenix

"The result of taking Memento and making it gentler, funnier, and yet infinitely more heartbreaking... a talented poet, Gee sometimes has the dialogue of the many characters he nimbly portrays echo with an almost lyrical resonance." Entertainment World, Canada

"Lovely and rather hilarious... the unraveling of the crime proves delightfully clever." The Marble, Victoria

"The audience is masterfully misled by likely suspects, motives, red herrings and perfect alibis... the tying together of plot strands is as satisfying as it is commanding. It's a rollercoaster ride without shock absorbers." Sabotage, UK

"Remarkable... riveting in his dialogue and empathic in his characterisations, bringing warmth and humour to a subject that could be played crassly in other hands... fiercely funny, heartbreaking and very much a must-see." Edmonton Journal, Alberta

"Gee has struck gold in conceiving this unique and compelling piece of one-man theatre... the writing is superb. Some is pure poetry, other parts are comic genius." Daily Info, Oxford

"Hilarious and heartbreaking... a brilliant plot." Victoria Times Colonist

"(Gee) has combined comedy and social commentary in a show that's sometimes hysterical, sometimes heartbreaking, always kind... I laughed a lot and shed a few tears." Mooney On Theatre, Toronto

"Entertaining front to back, wonderfully written, and brilliantly executed... this look into the world of dementia is unique and almost a relief in the midst of so many stories regarding this disease." CFUV Radio, Victoria

"Unique and hilarious... gut-splitting and heart-melting... no amount of hype could have prepared me for this show... I was completely blown away." The Jenny Revue, Winnipeg

"The fact that Gee makes comedy out of this and still manages to treat his subjects with respect is remarkable... in one story by one performer we have at least ten colourful characters, three different side plots, hilarious comedy and thought-provoking drama. You couldn't ask for more." Edmonton Sun, Alberta

"One of the most well-known and beloved artists on the world fringe circuit... devilishly delightful... heart wrenching and beautiful." Calgary Herald

"A tour de force... a one-man mashup of Memento and Clue." Orlando Weekly

"Silly, entertaining and eye-opening, this is terrific theatre." Vancouver Sun

By Rob Gee

Kevin, King of Egypt
My Daughter is a Donington Goth
Pig on the Wall
The Day My Head Exploded – Poems About Healthcare

Further details

mantlelanepress.co.uk or robgee.co.uk

Forget Me Not

The Alzheimer's Whodunnit

by

Rob Gee

First Published in the UK in 2016 by Mantle Lane Press
Third edition 2019

ISBN 978-1-9998416-7-6

Mantle Lane Press
Mantle Arts
Springboard Centre
Mantle Lane
Coalville
LE67 3DW
www.mantlelanepress.co.uk

Printed and bound in the UK by Imprint Digital,
Upton Pyne, Exeter, EX5 5HY

Cover design and interior layout Matthew Pegg
www.mpegg.co.uk

For Tommy

CONTENTS

Foreword

Rob Gee qualified as a psychiatric nurse in 1994 and worked for twelve years in psychiatric units around the UK and Australia. Working mainly in general psychiatry, he has also worked in child and adolescent units, drug and alcohol services, dementia wards, eating disorders, early psychosis intervention and psychiatric intensive care.

Now a performance poet, Rob tours internationally and has won numerous poetry slams, including The Edinburgh Slam, The Arts Council's Lit Up Slam, BBC2's Why Poetry Matters Slam and the Orlando Poetry Smackdown. He's won over twenty awards for his solo shows and regularly leads comedy and poetry workshops in mental health settings. He is patron of Leicester Action for Mental Health Project (LAMP) and lead artist for BrightSparks Comedy Asylum.

Forget Me Not is set on a substandard elderly Challenging Behaviour ward in the mid-1990s. A great deal has improved since then, but it's still the people with the worst memory problems who tend to be the most forgotten about.

Several stories depicted in the show are true, except the murders, obviously. However, for reasons of confidentiality and respect, the characters are all fictitious.

Author's Note

Forget Me Not was recently adapted and performed by a theatre company of retired people in Winnipeg. I was subsequently treated to dinner by them and had the delightful experience of the cast members all introducing themselves to me in character. It was so surreal that, to this day, I'm not entirely sure that it actually happened.

With my permission, they had adapted the show for a twelve-person cast, removing some lines and adding others as they felt necessary. Because they could now show rather than tell, several scenes were re-written accordingly.

This made me realise that much of this text was written for my particular delivery as a solo performer. I therefore want to emphasise that if you do find yourself performing it, feel free to alter the lines (not the plot, mind) in a way that allows you to put your own personal stamp on the characters. I've also added some lines that I was originally obliged to delete in order to fit the show into sixty minutes. Needless to say, they're optional.

Rob Gee,

August 2017

Characters
In Order of Appearance

Elsie	A retired nurse who realises she's losing the plot.
Dean	A nurse. Not the sharpest tool in the box, but his heart is good.
Andrito	An aggressive war veteran with dementia and liver failure.
Jim	A determined widower facing an ominous diagnosis of his own.
Timothy	A nurse who loves birds and lives with his mum.
Molly	An ex-Sunday school superintendant who repeats herself all day.
Percy	A bewildered old man in a constant state of arousal.
Percy's Wife	She doesn't visit very much.
Janet	The ward manager. A nasty piece of work.
Claudine	A burned out nurse with several decades of clinical experience.
Eric	An ex-scholar who may or may not think Timothy is his manservant.
Old Fella	A confused gentleman who loves his wife.
Old Fella's Wife	She loves him back.
DI Rae	The baffling police detective.
Pathologist	He or she is very helpful.

Prologue

Elsie:

To whom it may concern,

I've never been known for my attention span.
In fact my husband thinks I'm gormless;
but I'm losing my memory one story at a time.

And at the moment I'm getting away with it
in a forgetful kind of way.
I'm trying to keep things in the front of my mind
and I've only left the gas on a couple of times
so far,
that I'm aware of
today.

Now it just so happens that I spent a good chunk of my life
working as a nurse in dementia care,
so although I've no idea where it is my mind's going,
I'm under no illusions as to what's waiting when it gets there;

So I'd thought I'd better write this letter
for later on in my dementia,
and if you're the sorry sod who's reading it,
then my arse is your career.

I have half a sugar in my tea
and I'm very partial to custard.
I can't abide fisherman's pie,
especially when it's pre-digested.

You can swear in front of me
and I probably won't mind.
Don't worry if you're careless now and again,
as long as you're gentle and kind.
You can even take the piss a little if you like,
'cause I'll be giving you plenty of mine,

But don't treat me like an embarrassment,
even when I'm embarrassing.
Just keep me nicely medicated
and clap your hands if you see me singing.

Please don't manhandle me,
unless I hit you first.
Try and make sure I have clothes that fit me
and don't worry about being a brilliant nurse.
Just give me a lie in now and again;
and if I've filled my nappy but I appear quite happy,
change the other people first.

And please be patient with my husband.
We've been married since 1953
and every pore in his body is going to want to stay with me;
and although he'll be full of anger and pride,
he'll be quietly going to pieces inside,
so try and involve him as much as you can,
because he does do his best and he's only a man.

So thanks in advance
for all your hard work and dedication.
I hope I can make you smile as my senses slide,
and I hope that I'm a model patient.

I know the fact I'll lose my memory
won't stop me feeling things emotionally,
so smile a lot, have fun and lie to me;
and when I finally lose it all,
please give me somewhere soft to fall,
so I can decompose with a modicum of dignity;
and if you have an ounce of compassion,
try and slip me the occasional whiskey.

I think that completes the briefing.
I wish you well in all you do,
and if ever you're in my position,
I hope someone does the same for you.

Cropswood Challenging
Behaviour Unit

Saint Clement's Hospital

Spring 1994

Scene One

Dean:

So the way we keep them on the ward is what we call the Baffle Lock, and it's brilliant. You see we can't lock them in, 'cause technically they're all voluntary patients, but we can't let them go either, 'cause they're proper mental; so to get round it, the Baffle Lock... it's just two door handles, basically. There's one in the normal place and another one at the top of the door; so to open the door, all you do is turn both door handles and you're through.

Now, if you've got late stage Alzheimer's, what happens is you try the first door handle, which doesn't work, and then you see the one at the top; but by time you've seen the door handle up there, you've forgotten that there's a door handle down there. People spend hours; and each time it's a new thought in their head, so they're quite happy really. We get to bypass the Mental Health Act. Everyone's a winner.

Anyway, so Andrito – he's the Serbian fella, the one with the jaundice. Well, last week, he made it through the Baffle Lock; complete fluke.

Andrito:

(Shuffling through door with massive grin) Ah-haaa!

Dean:

Offski.

Half an hour later we notice the doors are open, so we do a head count and he's the only one missing; so we ring the police and give them a description, and they say "Alright, we'll go and find him and bring him back. We'll keep you posted."

Then I rang his wife. She wasn't impressed. She's going "Well I've looked after him for thirty years, you've had him less than a month and he's buggered off, well done." (Sighs and grins.) All in a day's work.

Anyway, about an hour later, we get a phone call from the police saying "It's all right, we've got him, we're bringing him back, we're about ten minutes away. We picked him up by the shops. He's in a bit of a state." Thank God for that. So I ring his wife. I say "Hello, just to say the police have rang, they've got him, they're bringing him back. He's in the back of their van."

And she says "No he isn't. He's here with me."

What had happened, she'd gone out in the car and found him, taken him home for a cup of tea; and the police had picked up this poor bloke. He's just an old fella out for a walk, matching the description; so he's in the back of the van in a right old state, and these coppers are going "Of course he's upset, he's mental!"

Quite a morning that was.

Scene Two

Jim:

Getting old is a bit like getting mugged, I think. You're
tootling along quite happily and it's as if someone pulls you
into an alley, they slap you about a bit, they pull your skin
so it's all baggy and loose, they pull your hair out – they're
particularly abusive to your prostate for some reason – and
then they chuck you back out onto the street, and you go,
Bloody hell, I'm eighty. I was sixteen last week.

She'd enjoyed the day hospital at first,
but she kept getting worse,
so they took her away
and put her in care:
a mock Tudor obelisk,
full of disinfectant and Stannah Stairlifts;
and that our life had come to this
was the hardest thing I've ever had to bear.

They said her behaviour was "challenging",
and, to be fair, it probably was.
She'd been with me forty years
and she was very much used to being the boss,

So they moved her to this other place,
which made her more confused,
and her behaviour got worse.

She punched the odd nurse,
so they finally sent her here;

And Elsie, my muse, best friend and mentor
faded so quickly. Now she's left me alone.
A part of me died when she first went away,
and I'll never forgive myself till my dying day
for letting them take her and put her in that home.

And now she's lying here with her life force finally spent.
She hasn't looked this peaceful since her memory first went.

The nurse explains how she fell and hit her head.
It had bled.
They'd made her comfortable and the doctor had come.
She was down as "Not for resus"
and without a great deal of fuss,
she quietly died
and there was nothing anyone could have done.

Then he says that maybe it's a blessing.
I look at him and he's actually smiling.
Maybe I should punch him.
I bet Elsie had a go.
Good on you, girl.

Can I have some time alone with her, do you think?

Dean:

Absolutely, yeah.
I'll just go over there.

23

Scene Three

Dean:

So we've got thirty patients,
all late stage dementia.
They've all got challenging behaviour;
and to deal with it,
we've got four nurses per shift.
That's one nurse per seven and a half doubly-incontinent
violent people.

We toilet them every four hours as a rule.
They all wear nappies
and they're always full.
The toileting, washing and feeding never really ends,
'cause by time you've done all thirty of them,
it's time to start again.

It's like a big smelly conveyor belt and I'm just a cog,
so I don't have to time to chat with this bloke
whose wife's just popped her clogs.

[My first day here, five years ago, I'll never forget it: I was a
fresh-faced student nurse. I walk into the lounge and the first
thing I see is this bloke, and he's naked as a pebble. He's quite
happy. And he's pissing into the pot plant. His aim's not that
good either…

(Mimes bloke swaying and urinating in a large arc, big grin)

Anyway, they sacked him.

Heh, you've got to make jokes or you just go daft.
I like a laugh.

They just suspended him.]*

Timothy:

Dean? Could help me with Molly? Her nappy's leaking.

Dean:

That's my colleague, Timothy.
He's been qualified for just over a year and he's a good lad.
Now and again we go out for a drink.
He likes bird watching, but I don't hold it against him.

Timothy:

Just hold her arms up for us. Cheers.

(Washing Molly and changing her nappy as he talks.)

So I finally got to see the Siberian Chiffchaff when it was
spotted near the sewage works at Bobbington. It's often
confused with the Willow Warbler, but it was definitely a
Chiffchaff, because it had the distinctive warm buff around
its supercilium. I've never seen one before, yet alone in such
intimate circumstances. It's the happiest I've felt since the
neighbour's cat died.

The sad thing is though, that the photographs were
overexposed. Yeah. I took the lens off and the blades of the

* Cut for performance

aperture were covered in oil, so I think the friction from the oil's viscosity impeded the speed of the closing action during exposure. Every silver lining has a cloud.

There you go, Molly. All clean and tidy, just like your wedding night.

Molly:

All day, all day, all day, all day…

Dean:

Lovely Molly.
It's been a very long time since she fell off her trolley.

She used to run the local Sunday school.
Apparently she was proper prim,
but then, when her brain started to shrink,
all the filth she'd spent years suppressing,
like fighting and spitting,
and swearing to herself for ages and ages,
throwing her zimmer frame at passing strangers,
taking all her clothes off in front of the chaplain
when he came to visit,
picking her nose, rolling it up and flicking it…
It all came to the surface,
as if, after a whole life devoted to the Lord,
she got terrified that heaven would just make her bored.

She used to be dead posh.
When she first came here, all she ever said was:

Molly:

Are you here all day, darling?

Dean:

And you'd go "Yeah," and she's say…

Molly:

Marvellous!

Dean:

Then two minutes later, she'd say it again.

Molly:

Are you here all day darling? Marvellous!

Dean:

She was so happy.
She'd say it to everyone all day long.

Molly:

Darling, are you here all day? All day? Marvellous.

Dean:

That was a couple of years ago, and now it's all gone.
All that's left now is just:

Molly:

All day, all day, all day, all day...

Dean:

But she's still happy.
And this is the thing:

If you are one of the lucky ones,
you can just regress and not be aware of it,
which I reckon is better than keeping all your marbles
and watching your body drop to bits.

Take Percy:
one of the happiest people I've ever met;
a patient of exceptional quality.
He's in a really good mood and he's always horny.
It's amazing.
He'd get sexually aroused by a brick.

Percy:

Show us your boobs, show us your boobs, guarrrn! Let me feel
your boobs, gu-arrrrn, gis a poke, gis a poke...

Dean:

Aw Perce, I'm a bloke.

Percy's wife doesn't visit very often:

Percy's Wife:

I've known him sixty years and he hasn't interested me once.

Dean:

I take him past Janet, our ward manager.
She's got a face like a gonad that's just been stamped on.
She hates it here.
She's particularly upset today,
'cause she had to help Timothy give out the tablets earlier,
which meant talking to patients.

Percy makes eye contact.

Percy:

Phooaarrr... Are you with me tonight?

Janet:

Get him out of my sight.

Scene Four

Janet:

Sorry to keep you waiting, Mr Barson. My name's Janet
Musgrove, I'm the ward manager here. My condolences about
your wife, still it's probably a blessing. For what it's worth,
I gave her her tablets earlier and there were plenty of them.
I'm sure she died without a great deal of pain. Now was there
something you wanted?

Jim:

Janet Musgrove? I'll just write it down. Sorry. My memory's
not what it used to be these days. So Elsie fell over?

Janet:

Yes, Mr Barson, falls do happen to people your age.

Jim:

It's true, that. I can't even sit on the floor without falling off.
Mind you, for her age, Elsie was alarmingly sprightly,
which was why the other places struggled to cope with her,
so I must confess,
I'm a little bit perplexed
as to how she came to fall over.

Janet:

These things happen, Mr Barson.

Look, we followed the appropriate procedure,
and informed the shift coordinator
for the hospital, who today happens to be me.
I informed the police surgeon and he was quite happy.
It was documented quite clearly
that she was not for resuscitation,
so leaving aside the fact she's dead, I really don't see a problem.

Jim:

Well the nurse… (Looks at notebook)
… Dean…
he let me have some time alone with her,
and I noticed there were some red marks on her arms,
as if she'd been grabbed or pushed.
They would have probably become bruises
if she'd lived for long enough.

Janet:

Mr Barson,
this is a Challenging Behaviour ward for people with dementia.
Our patients are completely gaga.
They've got the memories of goldfish.
Even if someone had grabbed her,
I can assure you they wouldn't remember it.

Jim:

Well, when I saw these marks, I had a look under her
fingernails; and under her right index finger I found a couple
of small hairs with a bit of skin attached. I've put them in my
glasses case. Here they are look.
(Pulls out case.)

Now, my eyesight's not what it was,
but if you look closely, you'll see that they're black.

Given that most of your patients have white hair,
this might indicate that whoever pushed Elsie
was a member of staff,
and, Elsie being quite a feisty customer,
she managed to fight back,
and she gave whoever did it some sort of scratch.

[(Jim accidentally sneezes into glasses case, both hairs are
lost forever).]*

Janet:

Hold on, stop! Okay?
I don't know what you're trying to imply,
but if we entertained every flight of fantasy
every time one of our patients died,
we'd be up to our necks in police and paperwork.

You were a police detective once, weren't you, Mr Barson?
Well you obviously miss it a great deal.

Jim:

Not in the slightest.
I always wanted to be a landscape artist.

There's something else. Sorry, hold on. (Looks down at
notebook)
... Her earrings have gone.

* Cut for performance

The nurse, (Looks down at notebook)
... Dean...
He gave me a bag of all Elsie's things and they're not in there.
They're terribly important to me.
I was wondering if you'd seen them anywhere?

Janet:

I'll keep an eye out, Mr Barson. Now I really do have things
to be getting on with. By the way, my condolences about
your other news. You know – about you being diagnosed with
Alzheimer's? Sorry, had you forgotten? Anyway, I'm Janet
Musgrove, ward manager. Goodbye, Mr Barson. You have an
excellent future.

Jim:

She stands up. She's got black hair and there's a very recent
scratch on the back of her neck.

That was important for some reason.

Scene Five

Dean:

Claudine and Claudia have worked here for decades,
and they're so burned out it's unbelievable.
They've got the interpersonal skills of a farting gerbil.

Claudine:

Hey Dean!
Andrito's punching Eric.
Sort it out.
I've just sat down.
Well, I'm about to.
Claudia's on her break.
You can disturb her if you like,
but I wouldn't do that if I were you.

Dean:

Andrito – he's the bloke with the jaundice;
the Serbian fella who made it through the Baffle Lock
last week.

Now him and Eric have got nothing in common.
Eric was an academic who studied the Italian Romantics.
Andrito killed people when he fought for the Chetniks
as a kid in the Second World War.
He then got plastered for the rest of his life

to help him deal with all the stuff that he saw.
He's got chronic liver failure and his skin is all yellow,
but age hasn't caused his demons to mellow.

Andrito:

De de fe fe defa leg de fa!

Dean:

I don't know what he's saying.
We thought he'd gone back to speaking Serbian,
but then his family came over
and said "No, we can't understand it either,"
so it's bollocks, basically;

But he's not very happy
and he's built like a haystack,
and his skin might be yellow,
but his hair is jet black.
He's just bumped into Eric and given him a slap.

Eric:

No, what are you doing? Can't you see?
I'm Alexander the Great sitting on a rock!

Dean:

Eric is trapped in his own mental prison.
It's impossible to tell
whether he thinks he is Alexander the Great,
or that's just one of his fancy euphemisms.

Timothy's straight in:

Timothy:

Eric, come with me, there's something really interesting on the telly.

Eric:

Ubezio, no! You bring only trouble with you!

Dean:

Eric always calls Timothy 'Ubezio'. The real Ubezio was Eric's manservant when he lived in Italy. While Eric was being all clever and academic, it was Ubezio's job to follow him around, nagging him about his personal hygiene and reminding him to eat and shave and change his underpants and stuff like that; which is pretty much what Timothy does with him now.

So again, it's impossible to tell if Eric actually thinks Timothy is Ubezio, or if he just calls him that 'cause he thinks he's a massive pain in the arse.

[Percy:

Hey, show us yer boobs...

Dean:

Percy shuffles past us with his trousers round his ankles, flashing his knackers to anyone who wants an eyeful. He's trailing a soaking nappy behind him.

Percy:

Tonight's the night, tonight's the night!

Dean:

So we abandon the pair of them and toilet Percy instead.
It's only half past five and I'm ready for my bed.]*

In thirty minutes they've all got to be fed.
It's only half past five and I'm ready for my bed.

* Cut for performance

Scene Six

Jim:

I wish I could remember all the things that I forgot,
but I'll never forget how to pick a lock;
so now I'm in the staff room, which is a little bit naughty,
and if Elsie was here, she'd probably tell me off,
but someone's up to something and, likely as not,
something in one of these lockers could help me
work out what.

Dean... (looks through notebook)
He's the nurse who showed me Elsie's body.
I've written in here that he's a bit too jolly.
He's what the boys at the station would have called
"A bit of a tit".

(Opens Dean's locker)

He's got half a bag of popcorn,
some stationary he's probably nicked,
and a magazine about cars,
with a half-naked lady on it.

Who else is on duty? (Looks at notebook.)
Timothy.

(Opens Timothy's locker)

Not much in his locker:
some digestive biscuits; last month's rota,
and a letter.

(Opens letter)

"In strictest professional confidence.
Thank you for your enquiry, etc etc.
Timothy Green has worked here for just over a year
and I've found his level of competence to be acceptable,
although nobody really likes him
and he's not very professional.
Don't hesitate to get in touch if you need anything further.
Yours sincerely, Janet Musgrove, Ward Manager."

(Puts letter in pocket)

Janet Musgrove.
What's in your locker?

(Opens Janet's locker)

Bunch of papers; jobs bulletin.
She's circled all the positions she's interested in.

Then I see them:
two sterling silver diamond stud earrings.
The ones I bought Elsie for our silver wedding.

I need to get out of here and write this down before…
Oh dear.
Someone's opening the door.

Scene Seven

Dean:

Andrito has now punched Timothy. He'd filled his nappy and
Timothy was trying to change him on his own; which is never
a good idea, especially if you're Timothy:

Timothy:

Okay, Andrito, I'm just going to take you into this toilet and
pull your trousers down. Okay?

Dean:

So Andrito gets the wrong end of the stick, so to speak,
and punches Timothy on the nose.
Now Timothy's got blood and snot all over his clothes.
I've just paged Janet, the ward manager,
and broke the news to Timothy that he needs to go home.

Eric follows us all the way to the staff room door.

Eric:

Ubezio, the swine you are!

Dean:

So we walk into the staff room
and there's Elsie's husband

standing by the lockers
looking all confused.
Poor old sod.
Apparently he's got Alzheimer's too.
Early stages, but, you know,
what can you do?

Mr Barson? I thought you'd gone home.
You're not allowed in here.
Yeah alright. Cheerio.

Timothy gets his stuff together and leaves.

Timothy:

Good bye.

Dean:

I walk Elsie's husband to the staff room door,
and tactfully remind him his wife's died.

He asks who found her.
Timothy found her.
He gave her her tablets earlier,
and then he got all worried
that she was a bit unsteady on her feet.
Half an hour later, he goes back to check
and finds her lying there with blood coming out her head.

Elsie's husband starts writing in this little notebook
and then he asks me if I think Timothy might have pushed her.

Timothy's not the kind of person that would do that to someone,

although to be fair,
he is forty and he does live with his mum,
so he probably has a murderer's profile...

Anyway, things to do. Toodle-loo.

So now we're down to three of us for the rest of the shift:
Me, Claudine and Claudia.
Janet's coordinating the shift for the hospital,
but she's going to have to come back here and chip in.
That'll make her happy.

(Claudine bursts in:)

Claudine:

Dean! Andrito's gone missing again. You need to go round the
hospital grounds and look for him; and give his wife a ring and
do an incident form and tell the police.
Me and Claudia, we'll keep an eye on the ward.
Well what are you waiting for? Today please!

Scene Eight

Jim:

Elsie's dead and it hasn't sunk in.
I've already spent five years grieving.
Maybe I've run out of grief.
I wish I didn't feel so relieved.

I'm in the lounge writing everything down.
My memory's not what it used to be.

Next to me an old fella's talking with his visitor:

Old Fella:

If you don't mind me saying,
I do think you're awfully nice.
I wonder (kneels on one knee with some difficulty)
would you do me the honour of becoming my wife?

Jim:

She looks at him and smiles.

Visitor:

I am your wife. We've been married quite a while.

Old Fella:

Oh. Is this a conjugal visit?
We should have kids.

Visitor:

We do have kids! Margaret's sixty-one and Harold's sixty-three.

Old Fella:

Oh. Are they behaving themselves?

Visitor:

I hope not.

Jim:

She kisses him,
just as a nurse walks in.

Claudine:

Mr Barson? Word to the wise:
Our ward manager has nicked your wife's earrings,
but you didn't hear it from no mouth of mine.
I ain't no whistle blower,
but they definitely went missing after she was alone with her;
and she'll deny it if you ask her,
so you need to write a letter.
Then at least she'll know that people are on to her.
It's worth a try.
Anyway, those arses won't wipe themselves, got to go. Bye.

Jim:

And she's gone.
I carry on writing.
Then the other nurse walks in:

Dean:

Anyone seen Andrito?
[Big bloke, yellow skin, black hair –
looks like a bee?]*

He's been gone for nearly an hour.
I've looked all round the hospital grounds,
Janet still hasn't answered her pager.
Claudine's gone to her office to leave a note on her desk
asking her to pull her finger out of her orifice,
while I've got to do the crap job.
I'm really not looking forward to this.

(Picks up phone, dials)

Hi, is that Mrs Novačić?
It's Dean from the ward. Hello.
It's about your husband.
Yeah, I'm afraid so.

Well, he punched a nurse about an hour ago,
so he was definitely here then.
We think he's gone through the Baffle Lock again.
Anyway, sorry about that.

Please don't shout, Mrs Novačić, no, please don't cry.
Okay then, nice to talk to you, see you soon then, bye!
(Hangs up.)

That went well.
Claudine appears, looking green around the jowls.

* Cut for performance

Claudine:

Dean, quick, Janet's office, now!

Jim:

The nurses run out of their office as if their tails are on fire.
I might as well go after them.
I won't find anything out by staying here.

We go through some corridors and a couple of doors.
Eventually we reach another office, and lying on the floor
in a pool of blood, looking distinctly dead
is...

(Looks at notebook, looks up again)

... Janet Musgrove, ward manager.
Someone's evidently bashed her head
in; and standing over her, holding a paper weight,
is a very angry looking yellow skinned dark haired patient.

Scene Nine

Claudine:

Dean! Your gob's hanging open like a half-baked fish!
Pull yourself together,
and if you can't, get Claudia!

Hi, Andrito. How are you?
Now I'm moving very slowly, and all I'm going to do
is take this paperweight off you and put it down.
There.

Now come with us.
We'll take you to that room
with the mattress on the floor.
We'll leave you in there, lock the door,
and you can have a rest.
Try not to slip on the blood.
Dean's going to hold your other arm.

(Waits patiently, eventually yells:) Dean!
There you go.
Very good.

Dean:

How can she be so bloody calm?
It's almost as if she expected to find Janet dead all along.

We take Andrito away from Janet's body,
out of her office, past Elsie's husband.
Hold on, what are you doing here?

Jim:

To be perfectly honest, I've no idea.

They look at me
and then off they go
with the patient in tow.
Looks like I've got a crime scene all to myself,
and there's a box of rubber gloves on the shelf
by the window.

The papers on her desk are in a mess,
as if someone's been going through them.
In her out tray is a single envelope.
Probably the last letter she ever wrote.

(Opens letter)

"In strictest professional confidence.
Thank you for your enquiry, etc etc.
I have no hesitation in recommending Timothy Green…
excellent nurse… punctual, reliable,
extremely professional… asset to the team…
don't hesitate to get in touch if there's anything further.
Yours sincerely, Janet Musgrove, Ward Manager."

Sounds like this Timothy's an excellent nurse.

(Puts letter in pocket, bends down, looks at body)

Major head trauma.
And her watch has been broken,
as if she raised an arm to defend herself.
The time on it says twenty-six minutes past six.
She's been dead for exactly thirteen minutes.
The blood around her head is starting to congeal.

(Looks around)

This doesn't make sense.

I look closely at the watch again,
and I realise exactly what happened.
Oh my God.
Where's my pen?

Scene Ten

DI Rae:

Well it's as plain as the egg on your face
that the person who did this is still on the ward,
so if we step up to the plate and lay our cards on the table,
grab the bull by the proverbial horns
and run somewhere with it,
then we can establish beyond any question of doubt
what seems to have happened.
The early bird is worth two in the bush,
so let's get our ears to the ground and see what comes up.

Ah. Mr Barson.
I'm Detective Inspector Rae.
This is my colleague, Detective Sergeant Mears.
You probably won't remember me from your days as a detective.
I was in uniform back then and still green behind the ears.
We've been interviewing everyone on the ward
and having a look to see what we can hear.

We need to sit down and walk through a few things.
I'm going to stick my neck out on a limb
and cut straight to the wild goose chase.
Rest assured my mind is currently an open slate.

Now, as an ex-detective chief inspector,
it seems you've got a chip off the old block on your shoulder,

and you've spent the whole evening poking around,
but now the foot's on the other hand,
and I hate to be a spanner in the ointment,
but I have to ask you to leave off,
because I don't want you interfering
with the good work that we're doing,
and too many cooks gather no moss.

I'm sorry to hear about the death of your wife.
The only thing I can advise
is to try and keep a stiff upper chin.
Everything points to the ward manager being done in
by the patient with the paper weight.
Although he has a brain the size of a grape
and can't take responsibility,
we do need to make sure we have our Ps and Qs crossed
before we take him into custody.

He scratched the deceased on her neck earlier today,
when she gave him his medication.
He was then found standing over her
holding the murder weapon,
so when you boil it down to its nuts and bolts,
it really isn't rocket surgery,

So I don't want you stepping on anyone else's thunder,
and if you interfere in any way, you'll be skating on hot water.
We'll be watching you with a fine toothcomb from now on.
Do you follow where I'm coming from?

Scene Eleven

Dean:

Well. They were going to evacuate the ward,
but the patients are all too bonkers to go anywhere,
so instead we're in lock down,
and all of us have to stay in the lounge.

Claudine and Claudia are whispering to each other.
Molly's saying "All day, all day, all day" to all the patients.
Eric's chuntering on about Ubezio,
but he's not being any bother.
Percy's just showed his penis to a burly police sergeant.

I rang Timothy at home and begged him to come back,
'cause it's only his nose,
and what with Janet being dead, we are short of staff.

Timothy:

Well I'm here, but it's under sufferance. Time Team was just
getting to the exciting part.

Dean:

[The scene of crime people are doing their thing
in white all-in-ones, coming and going.
They've got hoods and masks.
They've hijacked the ward.

One of them walks straight past us with his nose in the air,
up to the ward door;
and he can't open it.
It's the Baffle Lock.

Scene of Crime Officer:

Fuck's sake…

Timothy:

Shall we tell him about the door handle on the top?

Dean:

Maybe we should in a couple of minutes,
but in the meantime, let's just watch for a bit.]*

A couple of coppers come up to me.
It's time to take Andrito into custody.
I've got the key to the seclusion room, so I go with them.

It's a bit quiet.
He made a right racket when we put him in there.

I put the key in the door.
I get my eye up to the hole, just to be sure…

Where's Andrito?
Where did he go?
There's a massive pool of blood on the floor.
Oh no!

* Cut for performance

Scene Twelve

DI Rae:

Well this is great.
We've bitten off the wrong end of the stick
and now they're dying like hot cakes.

So three people have died on this ward this evening,
and if we think it's a coincidence,
we'll be up shit creek without a pot to piss in.

So maybe there is a connection to Elsie's death.
The chaps are in the mortuary looking closely into her head,
and our pathologist is with the patient in the seclusion room,
just to make sure that he's definitely dead.

So without jumping to… straws,
let's look at all the people with probable cause:

First – Timothy: the nurse with the plaster on his nose
who lives with his mum.
He was sent home and seen there by his neighbours
at the exact time the ward manager's murder was done.

He was sent home by his colleague, Dean,
who might have wanted him out of the way.
Dean was the only person
who had the key to the seclusion room;

but we've kept everyone in the lounge since we arrived here,
so he couldn't have gone in there and killed the old man,
unless of course he's some sort of ninja.
And I'm not convinced he's got the skills for it.
Personally I think he's a bit of a tit.

Then there's the other two nurses, Claudine and Claudia.
They were left to their own devices
while Dean was off the ward looking for Andrito,
so either of them could have killed the ward manager incognito
and then put the paperweight in Andrito's hand;

And, if they were working as a team,
one of them could have distracted our officers,
while the other one somehow managed to get into the
seclusion room and bump him off;
so they might have had the means, but the sad fact is
we've kept our ears to the grindstone and we're stumped for a
motive.

Then there's the patients:
There's Eric, who calls Timothy "Ubezio".
He was attacked earlier today by Andrito.
Molly, who says "All day, all day, all day"
... all day
and rocks a lot;
and Percy,
who might yet stab us all to death with his cock;

And there's another twenty-six of them
from whom we've not yet heard,
so we've not even scratched the surface
of the tip of that iceberg.

And then, Mr Barson, there's you.
Just follow the clues.
What would you be thinking if you were sitting in my shoes?

Now don't try pulling my leg over my eyes.
I think you blamed the Ward Manager
for the death of your wife,
so that gives us a motive.

You were in her office when her body was discovered.
You were then left there unattended,
where you had ample chance to destroy any evidence
that you were actually there thirteen minutes earlier,
committing the murder.

Also I've been informed
that you have the memory of a forget-me-not,
so how do you even know whether you did it or not?
This murder is so perfect you can even hide it from yourself.
Now that is how a murder should be done.
We know that you know how to pick a lock,
but how and why did you kill the old man in seclusion?

Jim:

I look at the detectives and then down at the floor.
What did I come in here for?

The pathologist walks in.

Pathologist:

Hello, everyone. The dead old man in the locked room:
after a cursory inspection, my distinct impression

is that he died of esophageal varices:
natural causes; it's a drinker's disease.

Basically the blood supply to your liver gets slowed,
which causes the veins in your oesophagus to swell up,
and sooner or later they just explode
without warning,
and then you die from all the endless haemorrhaging.

This happens quite a lot with liver damage,
particularly cirrhosis,
and if you look at his body, he was clearly very jaundiced.
It could have been triggered
by the stress of him being put in the locked room.
It looks a lot more violent than it actually is.

DI Rae:

Well, that could save us burning the midnight oil at both ends.
If he died of natural causes,
then everything points back to him;
except for one thing:
we now know that the patients don't have access
to the ward manager's office, or that corridor,
so someone must have let him in.

Mr Barson, you are still a suspect,
but so are the rest of the nursing staff,
and I'm not inclined walk on eggshells before they hatch.
Let's get everyone together in one basket,
and see which one of them's the first to crack.

Scene Thirteen

DI Rae:

Now, as a team of highly dedicated nursing staff,
you'll all be very pleased
that we've left absolutely no stone un-squeezed
in our efforts to identity the killer of your ward manager.
Mr Barson has the clearest motive,
but he says he can't remember;
but we think he blamed her for the death of his missus,
and you can't make an omelette without burning a few bridges.

Jim:

I don't think I'm the kind of person that would kill a ward
manager,
but if I did, I would have had to have been extremely devious,
because I'd have known that it would be me
wanting to find out about it later.

(Expression changes as realisation kicks in)

Inspector,
if you'll allow me read though the notes that I wrote,
they might help us piece together the story.
and then maybe we can identify the murderer;
even if it's me.

(Pulls out notebook, looks through it.)

He mutters something
about clutching at the straw that broke the camel's back,
but I'm trying to concentrate.
It's not easy to decipher this dreadful handwriting,
but slowly, things do start to fit into place.

In fact,
I know exactly who committed this act.

… No, it's gone.
Sorry.
Just having you on.

Right. It starts when Elsie died after a fall.
Dean, you rang me and I came straight to the ward
to see her body.
It came as a surprise because she was always so sprightly.

There were marks on her arms and hairs under her fingernail,
as if she'd been pushed and fought back,
and given someone a scratch.

I tell the ward manager and she's somewhat dismissive,
but during the conversation
she said she saw Elsie earlier and gave her plenty of medication.

Later, in the staff room,
Dean tells me that Elsie's medication was given to
her by Timothy;
so it's distinctly possible that she was given double the dose,
which would account for her not being all that nimble on
her toes,

and if someone then pushed her to make sure she fell,
that would explain those marks and the hairs under her nail.

As to why I was in the staff room:
I was going through the lockers,
and I find the first of these two references…

(Takes references out of pocket, gives them to DI Rae)

The ward manager wrote it about Timothy.
It says he's the worst nurse in human history;
and this confused me,
because it's in strictest professional confidence,
from one employer to another,
so what was it doing in Timothy's locker?

Then the ward manager is found dead in her office.
I'd forgotten about the reference by then,
but I found this other one in her out tray.
It's about the same nurse.
In fact both references are completely identical,
except for the words,
and the signature's not the same,
so it's fair to assume that one of them is a fake.

DI Rae:

Hold on. Whatever did or didn't happen with the references,
the ward manager was killed at 6.26 exactly,
and we've confirmed that Timothy was at home at that time,
so put that in your pipe and smoke like a chimney.

Jim:

Ah yes. I think I've got an opinion about that.
Bear with me…

(Looks through notebook.)

We found the ward manager's body at 6.39,
which meant she'd have been dead for thirteen minutes,
according to the time on her watch,
which we all assumed had stopped
at the exact point of her murder.

The thing is
the blood around her head was already congealing,
so I couldn't help wondering
if she'd actually died significantly earlier;

So I looked again at the watch,
and if you look closely at the way it's been broken,
the smashed part is circular and right in the centre,
which is not consistent with a defensive action.
It's more like someone broke it on purpose.

And the only person who would do that
is someone who needed an alibi.
The same person who overmedicated my wife
and then pushed her over:
Timothy. You killed Elsie and the ward manager.
You then must have broken her watch and altered the time
to make it look like she'd died forty-five minutes later.

Then you took that patient into her office
and you managed to goad him into punching your nose.
You gave him the paperweight and left him there.
You showed your colleagues your injury and took yourself
home;

[When they noticed Andrito had gone again,
they assumed he'd done a runner,
which gave you time to get home and dry,
complete with the perfect alibi;]*

And he was in that office for nearly an hour,
without so much as the faintest idea as to the where or why,
and that made him the perfect fall guy.
He wasn't long for this world and, because of you,
he died confused and alone in an empty room.

Timothy:

This is ridiculous. You're a bewildered old man.
Your wife died earlier and I do understand
you're looking for someone to blame,
but I really need to go home, Inspector.
I'm supposed to be off sick and I'm sick of playing games.

DI Rae:

Hold on! Don't get your nipples in a twist.
Mr Barson might have hit the nail right between the eyes.
Do you have anything to say off the cuff of your head,
now he's destroyed your alibi?

Dean:

It's okay, Tim – I know you didn't do it,

* Cut for performance

and I've just had a brilliant idea that will get you out the shit.

When I sent you home,
you'd got all that blood and snot all over your clothes.
Well, a simple DNA test will prove conclusively
that all of it was from your own nose,
and none of it will be from Janet's head,
so you're completely home free.
There you go.
That's a pint you owe me.

Jim:

Timothy looks like someone's just kicked him in the testicles.
He looks at Dean, removes his spectacles,
and then he turns to me.

Timothy:

I never meant to hurt Elsie.
Janet always had it in for me.
She hated it here.
She couldn't get a job anywhere else and I was her scapegoat,
because I actually feel quite at home
working in a place like this.

Ask the rest of them.
None of them like it,
because it's completely unrewarding.
For them, it's just this endless rotation of feeding and toileting,
interrupted now and again by random acts of violence.
No one ever gets better or says thank you.
It's one of the hardest jobs anyone can do,
and Janet took all her frustrations out on me.

This was her playground and she was the bully.

So I applied for a job on the new assessment unit.
The interview went really well but then Janet said she'd ruin it,
by writing me the worst reference she could bring to mind.
She told me I'd be "granny farming" with her for the rest
of my life.

So in desperation I wrote my own reference
and switched it with hers.
I was scared they might contact her for verification,
but I thought if she was suspended for a major drug error,
she'd be off work for ages and that wouldn't happen;

So I told her I needed help with the tablets.
I'd been saving up some Valium.
Elsie was supposed to have two milligrams anyway,
and I thought an extra ten would put a smile on her face,

And if she fell over, it would then be investigated.
I'd report she was over-medicated.
It would be Janet's signature on the drugs card,
and she'd get the blame.

[I was genuinely trying to lower Elsie to the floor,
but she went and scratched me.
It really hurt.
I've got to hand it to her,
she was a feisty old bird;
so I ended up pushing her.]*

And when the fall killed Elsie I felt really rotten,

* Cut for performance

but I did hope at least her death might benefit
future patients, if it meant I could go to the assessment unit;
and Janet might even lose her registration;
but nothing happened. There was no investigation,
because when all was said and done,
Elsie was only a dementia patient.

And that's why I killed Janet:
because I needed to get out and because she deserved it;
and in killing her,
I've saved a lot of people a lot of misery,
but I never meant to hurt Elsie,
and for that, I'm sorry.

Jim:

[That's why you came back to the ward
when the police were called:
because I'd taken the real reference from your locker
and you'd panicked.]*

The sad thing is you could have easily got rid of Janet.
She was stealing off the patients,
and I have Elsie's earrings to prove it.

You did mean Elsie harm, because you pushed her over;
and you'd have got away with it if you'd left it there,
but then you killed someone who didn't have Alzheimer's
and that's when people cared.

DI Rae:

Well blow me down with a feather.
Timothy Green, you're under arrest.

* Cut for performance

You don't have to say anything, but it might harm your
defence if you do not mention, when questioned, something
you later rely on in court. Anything you do say may be given
in evidence. Do you understand?
Tell you what, it's a nasty looking scratch you've got there on
your hand…

Jim:

Well. I've solved one last murder,
just like the old days.
I can't wait to tell Elsie.
We'll go out tonight and celebrate.

As we walk out through the lounge,
an old man looks up at the nurse with the plaster on his face.

"Goodbye, Eric," says the nurse, as they take him away.
The old man silently watches him go.

Eric:

A rotten trick, worthy of Ubezio.

Epilogue

Dean:

As the years went by, all the rumours spread
about how I solved those murders.
It hasn't gone to my head.

I'm the ward manager now.
All the staff think I'm great,
because I'm less like a boss
and more like a socially inappropriate mate.

[Mr Barson – Elsie's husband –
now resides in a home nearby.
I sometimes go and visit him
and we both sit there giggling,
while he chatters at length with the ghost of his wife.]*

All the patients from back then are dead now,
except Molly,
who no longer says "All day, all day, all day…"
She just rocks quietly in her own gentle way;

And there seems to be a situation
with Horace, one of our newer patients.

It started when Molly fell over
and Horace helped her off the floor.
It was as if they'd never met before.

* Cut for performance

He took her into the lounge and they sat together
and they couldn't take their eyes off each other.

A couple of days later they did it again
and now they do it all the time.
Neither of them have any kind of memory,
so every time they meet it's love at first sight.

Sometimes they hold hands.
Sometimes they actually kiss.
One day they were full on snogging,
but we pretended not to notice.

Maybe love does conquer all –
we just don't know why or when.
They enjoy each moment for what it is.
It's all sort of Zen.

And although Molly's mind can't memorise,
she doesn't really have to,
'cause you see it in her eyes;
and every day they meet and fall in love all over again.

Molly:

Are you here all day?
Marvellous.

Appendix

The Boxer

I try to hold the boxer's fists,
as he lashes out at my frame
with the fury that won his finest fights.

I hold him still,
whilst the nursing assistant tugs trousers to ankles
and wipes him by surprise with a vigorous towel.
He glares up at me with determination
and his fists vibrate in mine.
We briskly attach his braces.

His trousers bulge with piss-proof safety,
as he walk him into the lounge
and place him wobbling into his slumber chair,
where he will remain until nourished with pre-digested food,
washed down with Lactulose and a steel spoon.

We hold his fists and wipe his face,
as his coach mutters victory between the rounds.
He spits a mouthful of blood across the side of the ring,
towards the trophies at his bedside;
ageing, rigid and proud.
You can run your fingers through the dust
of the decades gone by,
the tears, joy and fights,
and Mother Nature rasps a tortured chuckle
as The Boxer tumbles from the ring,
collapses and submits.
Out for the count.

I don't understand how life can be so cruel
as to take away your hands
and leave you with your tools,
but if you look beneath the battered canvas,
a soul can be found
and just once in a while, it sings out loud
and you can see the former majesty
to which the trophies testify,
before it fades and disappears again,
as it atrophies and dies.

Every day in his mind, he's alone in that ring
punching out at his shadow.
The shadow always wins.

And as the scorecards hit the deck,
I thank my lucky stars,
because if he ever realised where he really was,
we'd have trouble on our hands.

May 1994

Mixed Metaphors

A selection of mixed metaphors that never made it into DI Rae's dialogue:

It's all spilt milk under the bridge.

I'm on the edge of the seat of my pants.

A little birdie told me that I have a gift horse in my throat.

We're beating around the bush with the wrong end of the stick.

I have a lot of black sheep in my closet.

They've cut the mustard from the same cloth.

He's not exactly a ray of roses.

We'll do this till the cows have come home to roost.

Don't flog a dead gift horse in the mouth.

I'm torn between a rock and the deep blue sea.

The fan is going to hit the roof.

Up a tree without a paddle.

Not until frozen pigs fly in hell.

There's always one rotten apple in the barrel of laughs.

Hopefully there'll be light at the end of the rainbow.

Don't bite the hand that rocks the cradle.

We'll burn that bridge when we come to it.

We've raised it to new depths.

Don't let the grass grow under a rolling stone.

He knew how to butter his nest.

He's not the sharpest marble in the drawer.

I can read her like an open can of worms.

I'd walk a mile in a camel's shoes to pass through the eye of a needle.

It sounds good on paper.

Just then, the fickle finger of fate reared its ugly head.

No use beating him over the head with a dead horse.

Grab the bull by the horns of a dilemma.

We can hang our heads high.

You can lead a gift horse to water, but you can't look him in the mouth.

If he told you to jump off a cliff, would you say, "how high?"

Don't count your chickens before you've cracked a few eggs.

Don't cross the road if you can't get out of the kitchen.

It's as easy as falling off a piece of cake.

Reporting Concerns

Forget Me Not is based on a 'challenging behaviour' elderly ward where I worked for two months as a student nurse in early 1990s. I left under a cloud after reporting some of what I saw.

A few years later I was working on an elderly ward in Melbourne, Australia. It was decent ward, although it was noticeable that some of the older nurses seemed to be slightly rougher with one particular patient in the way they washed, dressed and interacted with him. It turned out that around thirty years previously, this patient had been a particularly sadistic ward manager in charge of a dementia ward. Some of these nurses had worked under him and his whole situation now made them pretty chipper in a karmic kind of way.

I realised quite starkly that the way these nurses behaved towards this man was about them compensating for their guilt – none of them had done anything to protect their patients at a time when they were subject to the most abysmal cruelty at the hands of this individual. Their silence and collective compliance had allowed their ward manager to conduct himself in this way until he retired on a full pension.

Forget Me Not was written in the hope that more and more care staff are supported in speaking up to protect their patients, themselves and each other. The show has now been developed into a training package to assist staff from all areas of the healthcare spectrum in reporting concerns. I'm extremely grateful to everyone at Leicestershire Partnership NHS Trust for helping me to develop the training, as well as Arts Council England who funded the pilot sessions. Particular thanks go to Pauline Lewitt, LPT's Freedom to Speak Up Guardian, without whom the training would be a shadow of what it now is.

Areas for Discussion

The following questions are for professionals in health and social care, but can just as easily be considered by reading groups. Feel free to refer to the character list on page 13. Note: this page contains spoilers!

Elsie writes a letter to her future nurses outlining what she wants her care to look like when her dementia is more advanced. What would your letter have in it?

The story is set in the mid-1990s. What has changed since then? How is it different where you are?

What kind of nurse is Dean? Would you want to be nursed by him? Does he make a good ward manager?

What could Claudine have done about her suspicions that her line manager had stolen Elsie's earrings?

What do you think stopped her doing these things?

Timothy was being bullied by his ward manager. If you were Timothy what alternatives to murder would be open to you?

How can you create an environment where staff and patients alike are less likely to be mistreated by someone more powerful? What factors help maintain such an environment?

To enable this what needs to happen next:

- in your organisation?
- at your place of work?
- to you?

For training delivery contact Rob via robgee.co.uk.

Audio CD

Forget Me Not – The Alzheimer's Whodunnit

Written and performed by Rob Gee
Directed by Tara Gatherer

Recorded at The Planetarium, Winnipeg, Canada, July 2013
Recorded by Kayla Jeanson

Mastered by Neil Segrott at Tiny Studios, Leicester, UK
Thanks to everyone at the Winnipeg Fringe Theatre Festival

1. Prologue
2. The Baffle Lock
3. Elsie's Demise
4. Orientation
5. Jim vs Janet
6. Eric and Andrito
7. Staff Room
8. Man Down
9. The Lounge
10. No Andrito
11. The Body
12. Crime Scene
13. DI Rae
14. Lockdown
15. Accusation
16. Pathologist
17. Reveal
18. Exit
19. Epilogue

To listen online go to soundcloud.com/robgeepoetry